INTERVIEWS AND VIDEOS

Present Like a Pro and Nail That Job!

Gwyneth Letherbarrow MBA

CONTENTS

ACKNOWLEDGMENTS

Massive thanks to my sister, Alison Schenkl , for making sure that what I have written makes sense!

A SHORT STORY

At the end of 2012 I was holding a CV writing and interview skills workshop, and one of the participants told me that he was seriously worried about his future. The company he was working for was down-sizing, and because he was one of several people doing the same job, he was going to have to re-apply for his own position.

He was convinced that another colleague was going to get the job because they got on with the boss a lot better than he did, and he appeared close to despair. He worked hard at the workshop but I could see that there were a lot of questions for which he would still have to find the answers on his own, about himself, and about his employer.

About six months later when I was holding workshops on the same subject at the same company, I received a message during the coffee break that a young man had asked to talk to me.

At first I didn't recognize the person standing in front of me. He looked smart and confident, and had a huge smile on his face. "I got the job," he said, "thank you for changing my life."

I was amazed and overjoyed. This was the same young man who had previously seemed so close to giving up on himself. He told me that after the workshop he realised that he was responsible for his future, and had taken the time to step back, think about what he really wanted, what he could offer, and then spent a long time preparing his new image.

Back to the present day. Levels of unemployment are not likely to decrease drastically anywhere in the world any time soon. Society is on a mad upwards spiral, demanding that we have more and more academic qualifications, and yet we hear about an increasing number of graduates unable to find work.

Everywhere I go, people tell me that you "have to know someone" if you want to get a job, or "unemployment is so high, I don't stand a chance."

At the same time, if you look in the newspaper or on the internet you will see hundreds of vacancies, and some companies grumbling about the fact that they cannot find 'qualified' staff.

So what is happening? Technology is happening, workers' rights are happening, globalisation is happening, age discrimination is happening (even though the law says it is not allowed to happen), need I go on?

The undeniable truth, however, is that it is up to YOU to take action. There is no quick solution or magic formula, and there are no guarantees.

The content of this book is the same information and exercises that I use in training and private coaching, and I know that if you're prepared to invest in yourself, success will be yours.

And before you tell me that you don't have the relevant educational background, or that you come from a poor country, or that discrimination against women (or men) means that you are 'stuck', think again.

We all come to this planet with the same number of brain cells and the same abilities, and although our environment influences our beliefs, we can all choose whether to 'go for it', or to let life happen to us.

It's up to you as an individual to decide whether you're going to continue to look for excuses about why you're no good at interviews, or step into the brilliant being that you are!

There is a lot of work for you to do here because as a coach my approach to training involves asking a lot of questions, but I've made it easy for you by creating the simple to follow steps in this book.

My clients are testimony that if you are prepared to take the time to think and reflect about who you are and what it is you want, you will stand out far above the majority of other candidates, and you'll be a step closer to a fabulous and exciting future.

Good luck, you've got this!

INTRODUCTION

How do you feel when you get the notification that you have been selected for an interview? Inspired? Terrified? The biggest stumbling block that lets people down at interviews is nerves! And people are usually nervous because they haven't prepared properly.

You have done brilliantly to get your CV or application noticed, and it's really important to remember that you have the same chance of getting the job as all the other candidates who are invited for interview.

An interview is your opportunity to present and market yourself and sell yourself to your potential employer, and although your main aim is to make sure that you are selected for the job, it's also your chance to find out about the people you could be working for.

What if the job turns out to be the complete opposite of what you had expected? Let's say, for example, that you are going for an interview with a company that is located in a beautiful new building that has stunning views across the city.

You already imagine yourself looking through large windows, enjoying the sunshine in your office and having a sense of achievement.

You then find out at the interview that your office will be in the basement where there are no windows, no natural light, and you will have to sit there for eight hours a day without a lunch break.

Disappointed doesn't begin to describe how you might be feeling so remember that an interview is a two-way street.

Advances in technology have had a massive impact on recruitment practices in the past five years, and the days of having a quick chat with one or two people before being asked "when can you start?" are over.

For employers the recruitment process can be lengthy and expensive, and companies now include additional processes for finding out whether you are going to bring them value, before they meet you in person.

The newest (and very fast growing) trend is to ask potential candidates to answer a few questions on video, either using Skype or a specialist recording software such as Sonru.

Some companies invite candidates to work with other employees to resolve a problem, so that the manager can obtain feedback from everyone on the team about what they think of you.

You may be asked to give a presentation, or take a language or other technical test, or your potential employer may ask you to take some form of psychometric assessment.

So what can you do to make sure that you pass all these 'tests' and come out in one piece on the other side?

Preparation is paramount. I'm going to be repeating that fact throughout this book.

"By failing to prepare, you are preparing to fail" – Benjamin Franklin

If you have picked up this book, you have put yourself into the top 20 per cent of people applying for a job.

If you complete all the exercises in the book you will have catapulted yourself into the top five per cent of job applicants.

Why does that matter?

In my workshops I ask participants how long they spend on interview preparation, and their answers usually vary between a couple of hours during the evening before the interview, and a week's worth of evenings.

And that time is usually spent looking at the company website, or trying desperately to learn facts about projects, or technical processes, or policies ...

All that time is probably wasted however, because we have already established that if you have been invited for interview, you have the necessary qualifications and experience.

If you're an external candidate there is simply no way that you are going to be able to learn everything that goes on inside of the company, and if you're an internal candidate, you know more much than you think you do -

– and anyway, there are these things called computers that have huge memories so that you *don't* have to cram your brain full of facts that you might never use.

You have been asked to interview because the company or organization wants to meet YOU. They want to know how it's going to *feel* to work with you, to see you every morning, to find out whether your personality is likely to match the team already there.

The problem is as follows: very few people feel comfortable when having to talk about themselves. When you were growing up you were probably taught that you shouldn't show off about your achievements because others would think that you were *big-headed* or *egotistical.*

Yet that is exactly the issue you must address, and in an age where competency based interviews are all the rage, this is a skill you cannot be without.

Your interview preparation should focus on you getting to know who YOU are, and because for most of your life you have been worrying more about what others are doing and what they might think of you, you have forgotten who the real you is.

You have been looking outwards, and to be successful at an interview you have to look inwards.

And now consider this: if you knew that the time in interview was the only thing standing between you and the job of your dreams, and that it could potentially change your life forever, how long would you spend preparing?

And would you be willing to put aside everything you have learned about not telling others how great you are?

And would you be willing to acknowledge that there is someone quite brilliant inside of you?

Once you are familiar with what is great about you, you can learn to market and sell yourself without feeling awkward or embarrassed. You will also discover that the only person in control of you is you.

You can decide how to answer the interview questions.

You can choose how to behave on camera or in person.

No-one else can make you do or feel anything you do not want to.

The third edition of this book includes a chapter dedicated to interviews on video, with answers (kindly provided by Sonru) to the most frequently asked questions I hear from my clients and which will help you to present like a pro.

By following the steps and completing the exercises in this book you will have *automatically reduced your stress levels* and have a fantastic interview.

Get yourself a notebook or journal, and write your notes using a pen. Typing on a laptop or tablet or 'phone encourages your brain to focus on getting the letters in the right order to make up the words –in other words, you're using your mechanical intelligence.

I want you to use your emotional intelligence, and by using a pen and paper you have a better chance of getting the creative juices flowing and getting some great ideas about how to formulate your answers.

One final note. It is never too early to start preparing for interview, even if you don't know when the next one will be. The most difficult questions you will ever have to answer will be those about you, and the sooner you begin, the better.

Let us begin!

CHAPTER ONE - DECIDE

"Begin with the end in mind" – Stephen Covey

You have received notification that you have been selected for interview. Your first reaction might be a feeling of pure joy! The second reaction could quite well be a feeling of doubt because of one of two (or both) things:

1.   You start questioning your ability to do the job for which you have applied because you are sure that all the other candidates are much better than you are; and/or

2.   you sent in your application without really thinking about whether you want the job, for example you told yourself that "the job looks interesting, let's give it a go and see what happens ..."

Stop right there!

If you answered 'yes' to the first statement, please remember that you have the same opportunity as everyone else. You have been invited to interview based upon the information you provided in your application.

I will challenge any person who suggests that they don't see the point in preparing for interview because someone else has allegedly already been selected.

Neither you nor the interview panel have any way of making a decision about who is going to get the job at this stage – and even if there is a preferred candidate (do you have evidence?), it's up to you to stand out so that there can only be one choice – YOU (more on this later).

If you answered "yes" to the second statement, you need to have a good think about your motivation for the application. Re-read the vacancy notice/job description and take note of what you are thinking and feeling as you go through the tasks and responsibilities.

When you get to interview and the question that will surely be asked, namely "why do you want this job", is posed, what will you reply? You may be desperate for a job so that you can pay the bills, but *before* you confirm your interview please consider the following:

1.　If this is a full-time job you could be spending a third of your life doing something you do not enjoy;

2.　you could be wasting everyone's time, including your own, if you accept the interview but have no intention of accepting the job (if offered);

3.　if you are offered the job and accept, you might be so miserable after two weeks or two months that you hand in your notice and start the job search process all over again;

4.　if you are offered the job and accept, you might not give your best, your performance could be lacking, and your employer decides to fire you after six months.

Employers want to know whether you are going to fit in with the team, whether you match their expectations, and whether you want the job.

Regardless of what you want to call it: intuition, sixth sense, gut instinct, etc., if you do not really *want* the job, the people interviewing you are going to pick up on the fact that something isn't quite right. They just probably won't be able to put their finger on what it is.

EXERCISE

Write down every reason you have for *why* you want the job, because it is one of the most common questions to be asked and will contribute to how well you come across in your interview.

Your personal list may include the regular working hours, or travel time to work, or whether the company offers private health insurance. On a professional level you might think that the job looks interesting and will be good for your career.

Remember, however, that you are also going to have to look at the situation from the perspective of the person interviewing you. Why should they select you?

How will *they* benefit from your experience, and what do you have that no-one else can offer, or as some people might say, what is your 'unique selling point' (USP)?

We will take a closer look at other frequently asked questions in Chapter Three, and being clear on your motivation will make things easier later on.

CHAPTER TWO - IDENTITY

**"You were born to win, but to be a winner,
you must plan to win, prepare to win,
and expect to win" – Zig Ziglar**

Your CV has got you this far, and you have been successful in using it as a marketing tool to get you noticed. Give yourself a pat on the back, well done!

It may seem an obvious thing to remind you about, but you now need to ensure that you know your CV inside out, from back to front, and from top to bottom.

If you have applied for several positions, you will have to remind yourself of the vacancy notice and job description, and pick out all the examples of how you matched your experience to the requirements of this specific job.

Your CV is the document that the interview panel is going to use to verify some basic facts, so for example if you put down mountain climbing as a hobby, remember the name of the last mountain you climbed so that you can talk about it, if asked.

EXERCISE

Read your CV. Which strengths and skills have you highlighted? Write them down.

As already mentioned in Chapter One, employers want to know about your qualifications and skills, your experience and work background, but by far the most important reason for having an interview is to find out what sort of person you are.

Do you have a fun or serious personality? Are you going to be someone that your employer can rely on for long-term projects, or do you get bored easily and need variety?

You know that you are the answer to all their problems, but *the people interviewing you don't*, and you need to come up with some ideas to convince those people conducting the interview that you are their only choice. Look back at your answers in Chapter One. What else have you got to offer?

You may have heard about people getting a job for which they were not fully qualified. But the word 'qualified' can mean different things to different people. To you it might mean the level of academic achievement, to an employer it might mean that they believe you will fit in easily with the rest of the team.

Skills can always be taught, assuming you are willing to learn, but you will be setting yourself an unrealistic challenge if you think can change your personality to meet the demands of the job.

To give you an extreme example, I would not consider interviewing a rocket scientist for the position of a bank cashier, regardless of qualifications. These would clearly be two very different types of people.

But you want the job, right? So how are you going to make sure that the interview panel is so impressed with you that they completely forget about all other applicants? Do you believe in yourself?

Do you have your mind set on getting the job? If you want to 'click' with those interviewing you, you will also have to identify with them, and understand what it is that they want, and what their perfect employee will look like.

Read the vacancy notice and/or job description, and put yourself in the position of the employer. If you were the boss and the roles were reversed, what words would describe the person you were looking for?

Let me give you an example. One of my clients had applied to be a Mediator in conflict resolution. As we started his interview preparation he described himself as enthusiastic, dynamic and sociable. But those words didn't match the image of what a mediator should be.

Someone who is working at resolving conflict is more likely to be discrete, diplomatic and calm.

Go through the vacancy notice again and again.

- Which *key words* are mentioned the most, for example communication, or team player? These are words that you will include in your interview answers

- What are the top three tasks/responsibilities or competencies (because these are likely to be listed in order of importance) and how does your experience match them?

- What examples could you give to demonstrate that you can do those things brilliantly?

Do some detective work and go to the organization's or company's website.

- What type of language is being used? Formal or informal?

- If there are graphics of people, what type of clothes are they wearing?

- What is their mission statement?

- What was the subject of their most recent press release?

- When was their website last updated?

- Is there a biography/photograph of their CEO or Director-General? What impression do you have?

- Assuming you have the job, what will the first two weeks look like or feel like?

- What might you be doing? Where are you sitting? Who are you talking to?

Write down any thoughts that you have right at this moment because they will help you later on when you prepare your answers for the questions you will be asked at interview.

CHAPTER THREE - QUESTIONS

**"At the centre of your being you have the answer;
you know who you are,
and you know what you want." - Lao Tzu**

In 2013 I was having a conversation with some young people who had attended another training course on interview techniques, and was flabbergasted to hear that they had been told which answers to give; not about how to respond, but which words they should use.

If you were an employer holding interviews, how would you deal with candidates who all said the same thing? It's off-putting to say the least.

The internet is full of sites with information on what the best answers might be and it is undoubtedly helpful to research some ideas. But there is a good reason for you to refrain from simply memorizing what you think is a great answer.

You have been invited for interview so that the company you want to work for can get to know *you* (and not the person with the great answer taken from a website).

If you pretend to be someone else by giving clever answers that you found online, you may get away with it for a little while, but eventually your colleagues are going to realise that you aren't the person they thought you were. Not great for your credibility or integrity.

No-one said that preparing for an interview was going to be quick and easy, but the more prepared you are, the more confidence you will have, and the more confidence you have, the more in control you will be.

And if you have taken the time to prepare your own interview answers instead of using something you have taken from the internet, you will be able to adapt your responses much more easily.

As is the case when preparing your CV, at your interview you are going to have to paint a picture for the people that you are talking to, so that they can already *feel* what it's going to be like when you're working with them. It's all about marketing.

Let's talk about washing powder.

Washing powder (or liquid) manufacturers go to great lengths to persuade you to buy their product instead of a competitor's. Let's face it, these days most of them wash brilliantly at 20° and have fabulous technology that gets stains out first time around.

But you never see an advert where someone stands with a box (or bottle) of washing powder saying "this powder is great, you should buy it".

Instead you see a short film (advertisement) where the sun is shining, everyone is laughing and happy, the trees and the grass are a beautiful shade of green, the kitchen with the washing machine is spotless, and there are lines and lines of stunningly clean washing blowing in the gentle breeze...

The manufacturer is telling you that you too can have these incredible results and feel this amazing if you decide to buy their product.

It's the same when you are marketing or selling yourself.

How are you going to convince the interview panel that you are the washing powder that washes whites whiter than any other product?

I'm going to show you how. There are ten questions that you must have the answers to, and they are the ten questions that candidates most struggle with.

Take your time with this next exercise, be kind to yourself, and keep going back through what you have written until you feel comfortable with what you have.

As you are doing this work remember the following:

a)   For general questions (i.e., questions about you), aim to speak for between one and a half (minimum!) and three minutes when answering. Practise!

b)   Choose several real-life examples you can use to demonstrate your abilities because it is 'storytelling' that is going to help you to connect with your interviewers. Make sure that your examples are specific and that they are relevant to the position that you are interviewing for.

c)   If you are talking about an achievement or a great success, the example you give should ideally be as close to the present day as possible

d) If you are talking about your weaknesses or mistakes, the example you give should be as far in the past as possible.

e) If talking about team work, be careful to keep the focus on your own input. Bringing too many other people into your description (your picture) could cause the panel or interviewer to be distracted instead of concentrating on how great *you* are.

f) You will have already identified the key words from the job vacancy notice. It's a good idea to include these words in your answers to create a stronger connection with those interviewing you.

g) If you are an internal candidate, prepare as though you were coming from outside. Don't assume that your colleagues already know everything about you.

EXERCISE

Go through each of the following 10 questions. They may be phrased differently at interview, for example when talking about your greatest achievement your potential employer might be wanting to hear how well you worked in a team, or whether you follow through on tasks.

Remember that there are no right or wrong answers because there is only one of *you*.

Write your answers down as you go through the list.

1.   Tell us about yourself

What is your unique selling point? You have already considered this, but during the interview you will need to state over and over why the company or organization should hire you. This question is one of the most popular starts to an interview, and you must be clear about what sets you apart from others.

A common mistake is to begin listing everything that is on your CV or job application.

Remember that you have been invited to interview because on paper your profile matches the requirement of the job. This usually means that the people interviewing you are familiar with your educational background and work experience – so don't waste precious time telling them what they already know.

Write down all your strengths (skills) that you believe are relevant to the job. Then choose the three that are most important for the position and practise your answer.

For example, "As you can see from my CV/job application, I am an experienced project manager, and one of the reasons for my success is my background in accountancy and budgeting, because this means that I have learned how to keep project costs down through careful planning – for example, in my current/previous position (insert your relevant example) ..."

Depending on how much time you want to speak, do exactly the same with your other strengths.

Unless specifically asked, you shouldn't be giving long descriptions about your personal life, hobbies, and what you love to eat.

2. Why do you want this job?

Please note that your answer to this question will be very different to the *next* question on this list and you need to be clear about the difference when it comes to the big day.

What do *you* like about the company that you have applied to? What do they do that excites *you*? Is it a fast-paced business where you will be meeting lots of interesting people? Is it a company where you will be left alone to concentrate on your work?

Why are those things important to you?

Look back again at your notes and check whether there is anything else that *motivated* you to apply.

A great way to express your enthusiasm (your 'why') is to match tasks from your current position to the new job.

For example: "One of the things that I love in my current job is working in a team made up of different nationalities, and the fact that we all have a contribution to make for our common goals within a certain period of time, and I note that one of the key components in this (new) job is being able to work in a team environment where we have to meet tight deadlines ..."

Salary is not a great reason to give for wanting a job because everyone needs money and we all have to pay the bills. Do not mention personal benefits.

If and when you are offered the job, that will be the moment at which you can discuss holiday allowances and private health insurance.

3.   Why should we hire you?

How are you going to contribute? What qualities or skills do you have that make you special, and *why are they relevant* to the job? What makes you different to other candidates? What value can you give?

Whereas "why do you want the job" was about *your* enthusiasm for the company or organization, this question is about why your interviewer should be enthusiastic about you.

Let me give you a real-life example.

A client was applying for a senior legal position and was trying to work out what was different about her. After all, being a lawyer means following strict rules!

After some coaching she realised that one of her strengths was her approach to disciplinary cases, something that her current boss appreciated greatly.

Instead of simply presenting senior management with a pre-specified outcome in accordance with a certain breach of policy, she was able to look at the big picture, and suggest different ways of how the outcome could be reached.

In real terms that meant that if someone had done something so serious that it warranted them being removed from their job, she would present several options, which might include asking the staff member to resign instead of being fired.

What is it about *your* approach to your work that is going to make working with you an absolute pleasure? Again, pick two or three things from your experience that you do really well and that *match the requirements of the position.*

Remember to provide *relevant* examples – paint that picture in the minds of your interviewers! Help them to imagine that you are already doing the job brilliantly.

4. What did you enjoy most/least in your most recent job?

Focus on the positive and again, give examples that are *relevant* to the position that you are interviewing for. For example, if you loved pulling together information for reports, what was it specifically that you loved about the process? Was it because you could build strong working relationships with people from other departments? What else?

When talking about what you enjoyed the least, do not talk about other people or tasks that you didn't like, rather find something that this new job will provide that you didn't have before so that you can provide a positive comparison.

For example, you might look forward to shorter travel time to work, or working in a smaller/larger company.

5. Describe a problem that you successfully resolved/describe a time when you faced a difficulty/challenge ... OR when you made a mistake

Your answer is going to be made up of three parts:

a) What was the problem or mistake – acknowledge that it happened

b) How did you successfully resolve it? Which steps did you take?

c) What did you learn (so that it doesn't happen again)?

The most important thing when preparing to answer this question is to choose a problem that is not going to take a long time to describe, and that has a happy ending.

Talking about major difficulties in an attempt to show your magnificent problem-solving abilities can easily backfire on you. An interviewer would probably ask themselves why you hadn't done anything to prevent the issue getting to crisis point.

Focus on something that *you* had full control over, for example dealing with a customer complaint, or having to cut resources/costs, or re-shuffling the workload because of staff holidays, or even someone on your team missing a deadline for the weekly report.

Remember to choose an example that your interviewer is going to be able to identify with.

Here are five don'ts:

Don't tell the interviewer that you have experienced a lot of conflict.

Don't tell the interviewer that you have never experienced conflict.

Don't start off by saying 'well of course there is always going to be conflict at work.'

Don't mention job titles of those involved in the conflict because you don't know if the person you're talking about is the best friend/brother/sister etc., of someone on the interview panel.

Don't bring emotion into the conversation, for example "they were very angry with me," or "they were upset." Although it's a subject for another book, you will never be able to accurately judge what someone else is thinking or feeling.

Be confident and be factual, and use general labels such as 'colleague' (not supervisor).

6.   Describe your strengths/weaknesses

One person's strength is another person's weakness and I strongly advise you to stay clear of talking about personal characteristics.

The key here is to look once more at your skills. If you are serious about getting some feedback, ask your friends or family to tell you what they think you are good at and also what you aren't so good at. Remember though that you may not agree with what they tell you ...

On the upside, you may learn something new about how other people see you, which will be very valuable for your interview preparation.

Which strengths are going to be important for your potential employer? Are you quick to learn new computer programmes? Do you speak lots of languages? Are you great with numbers, or maybe you're fantastic at organizing events?

Choose two or three relevant core strengths and identify relevant examples so that when you get to interview, the only thing you have to be thinking about is which example to use.

Don't list – lists are boring and don't tell the interviewer anything about you.

When talking about your weaknesses focus on something skill-related (not personality-related).

Ideally you're going to choose something that is on the job description because if you are being interviewed, the person who invited you is clearly interested to see whether what you have to offer will make up for that shortfall.

You could say something along the lines of, "I see that the vacancy notice mentions five years of progressive work experience and I only have four, but as demonstrated when I started my current job, I'm very quick to adapt and to learn new things ..." or "I see that the job requires a knowledge of Oracle software, and whilst I haven't used it before, I'm quick to learn new things. For example, when I started my previous job ..."

Get the idea?

When talking about weaknesses always end with a positive statement.

7.   What do you know about the job/company/organization?

You would be amazed at the number of people who forget to research the company they want to work for. Unforgiveable. Look at the company's website. What is its mission statement? What are its values? From the language and pictures that are used, what sort of people do you think work there? Does it have regional offices and where are they?

What can you find out about the structure of the company and where your job might fit in? How many employees does it have? Are any press releases available that will tell you what its priorities are right now?

Does the company have a Facebook page or other social media accounts? Show the interview panel that you have done your homework. In so doing you will have already set yourself apart from more than half of the other candidates.

8.   Why do you want to leave your job/why did you leave your last job?

With this question your integrity is being tested. Are you going to criticise your previous boss or complain that you were bored? Absolutely not.

It's ok to want to move on and do something more challenging and interesting, but you have to convince the interviewer that you wanted to leave your other position for the right reasons.

How are you going to show them that you are reliable and can be trusted? Talk about the positive aspects of your last job, what you achieved there, and how you are now ready to try out your learning in a new environment. This is one of those questions that you should spend less time answering.

9.   We see that you do not have a lot of experience with sales/budgets/programming/ international relations (whatever); is that going to be a problem?

This is similar to the question about weaknesses and is testing your ability to think on your feet, as well as to find out how quickly you can adapt. When you applied for the job you will have seen the requirements of the position in the vacancy notice/advertisement, and so should already be aware if your CV does not fully meet all the criteria.

But, remember that *you* have been invited for interview, so there is something about *you* and your experience that is of interest.

The trick, therefore, is to turn such questions around, for example: "The question should not be 'is that going to be a problem', the question should be how quickly will I be able to learn about sales, etc.," – tell them how you are going to deal with that shortfall in your experience, and, without wanting to sound like a broken record, give your interviewer an example of how you dealt with a similar situation in the past.

10. Where do you see yourself five (or two or 10) years from now?

The interviewer wants to know what goals you have set yourself, and whether this job is just a stepping-stone for you to a higher position within the same company or somewhere else. Are you a goal-oriented person or someone who just wants to do the 9-5 and enjoy the salary? Well, what are your plans?

Other questions

There are hundreds of questions that might be asked, and many of them will be similar to those above, just phrased differently.

There are also some more unusual questions that pop up now and again, for example "if you were an animal what would you be", or "if you were a colour, what would you be".

I'm not sure how your answers to such questions will help the employer, but they will have their reasons. Remember that if you have included hobbies on your application, you must be prepared to talk about them.

What questions do you have?

Put together a check list of all the things that you want to know about the company so that you can go through them in your head as the interview progresses.

When you are asked at the end of the interview whether you have any questions, and depending on how you think the interview has been, you may want clarification on a couple of issues.

Acceptable questions might be:

1.   Could you describe to me what a typical day at the office looks like?

2.   Could you tell me why the last person left (unless it is a new position)?

3.   When might I expect to hear from you/when do you plan to make a decision?

Unacceptable questions are those:

1.   That concern personal benefits. The main aim of the interview is to market yourself to your potential employer. Salary and leave allowances can be discussed when you receive the job offer and not before. You should have done your research before you sent in your application.

2.   Concerning an issue that you should have researched before the interview, for example, what does the company do?

3.   If your question is of a technical nature and requires a longer explanation, are you sure that the interviewer is the right person to ask? Sometimes it is better to say that you have a question but that you will put it in writing after the interview.

This will take the pressure off the interviewer (who may not have the answer), and will also likely provide you with a better answer because the person writing it will (hopefully) have more time.

CHATER FOUR – BE A PRO ON VIDEO

"Proper Planning and Preparation Prevents Poor Performance" - Stephen Keague

Video is here to stay, and its use in recruitment will undoubtedly increase in 2017 and beyond because it allows a much more effective use of resources (both on an organisational and personal level).

Your greatest challenge is going to be to connect with someone who is not in the same room as you, because you are going to be talking to a camera on your laptop or computer, and depending on which software you're using (Skype, Sonru, etc.), the benefits of facial feedback and body language will be somewhere between minimal and zero.

For a large number of people, however, having to talk to a camera can bring up uncertainty, and in some cases pure panic.

I have heard hundreds of excuses from my clients about why they feel uncomfortable doing an interview on video, for example, 'my face looks fat', 'I'm too old', 'I don't have enough experience', 'I hate cameras' ...

But I want to tell you that you CAN present brilliantly *if you want to.*

By breaking down your preparation into three parts – Personal, Technical and Presentation – you will be able to better manage the process and reduce your nerves.

Let's begin by talking about how you can best connect with the human being that you cannot see.

1.   Personal:

Remember that you are being compared to an unknown number of applicants who are going to receive the same amount of time to answer the same questions.

Looking at a camera might make you nervous, but don't be tempted to start listing everything you have done. You need to grab the attention of the viewer in the first few seconds.

Hopefully the people watching your video will have read your job application and will know the number of years' experience you have and your current position. By repeating that information you will waste valuable time.

You must help the viewer 'feel' how it is going to be to work with you and to do that you must be able to market yourself in a way that doesn't appear aggressive or false.

Look at the '10 questions' I talked about in the previous chapter and work hard at making the connection between what you're doing now and the job that you're applying to.

Here's another short example of how to answer the question 'tell us why you want the job':

"One of the things I enjoy about my current position is the goals that we are working towards, because it's important to me to know that I'm making a difference … and reading the requirements for this job I get the feeling that there is a strong sense of purpose to helping others …"

I'm going to keep on saying this. It doesn't matter how well you know the people watching you on video. You are being *compared* to everyone else, and you must be able to stand out from the other applicants.

2. Technical preparation

Having the practical arrangements in place for your video interview could mean the difference between success and failure.

Check your internet connection, and confirm that your microphone is working. Although wireless connections (WLAN) are popular and may provide a good signal, if the signal drops for a few seconds, your recording could go wrong. If possible make sure that you are connected to the internet with a cable.

If you decide to record your interview at home, ensure that all family members have switched off the Wi-Fi on their 'phones or laptops/tablets, etc., because you want ALL the bandwidth. Again, get yourself a cable to connect to your router.

You may want to have a second laptop or computer, or mobile 'phone close by in case your system crashes (technology is wonderful but there are never any guarantees). Ensure that all your equipment is fully charged (and ideally plugged in).

Check your settings, including the volume on your microphone and whether you need to change the default devices for audio and video on your laptop/computer.

3. Presentation

If you are going to be using a programme that asks you to login to record your video, put time in your diary and stick to it. Check well in advance of the day where you are going to sit, as well as how your computer or laptop should be positioned so that your face and shoulders are showing.

If you decide that you need notes, ensure that your laptop or computer is positioned in front of a wall so that you can post notes *above* where the camera is positioned. In natural conversation we tend to look people in the eye (at their face) or sometimes we look upwards, and maybe to the side.

If you have your notes on the desk in front of you, you will be looking downwards, and you will lose the personal connection to the person watching your video. The same applies to when you look at the timer or something else on the screen. To the extent possible, talk to the camera lens.

Cut out a small circle out of a larger piece of paper so that if fits over your laptop/computer camera. This will help you to focus on the camera and not somewhere on your laptop screen (you can do the same for your mobile 'phone if you're using it to record).

Practise filming yourself and then play back the recording taking note of what you are doing with your hands, where you are looking, how you are sitting etc. You might also like to ask someone else to watch your recording to get some additional subjective feedback.

When you begin speaking, remember to smile, just as you would do when you met someone for the first time.

Recruitment via video is on the up and is fast becoming popular with organisations and businesses of all sizes, which is why I travelled to London to attend a conference hosted by Sonru, and where they kindly agreed to answer the most commonly asked questions on the subject:

1. <u>Where is the best place for me to be for my video interview recording (location)?</u>

The key to a good interview is to make sure you feel confident. You can choose the location where you complete your interview, which is a huge benefit! You don't have to worry about getting lost, missing your bus or turning up at the wrong office block. Pick the place where you feel most comfortable.

In our recent research on the candidate experience of video interviewing, it emerged that 86% of candidates completed their video interview from home. Wherever you choose to complete your interview, make sure you have a tidy, simple background behind you and that everyone knows to keep quiet. Don't let housemates, pets, deliveries or doorbells disturb you!

2. <u>What is better for recording the video interview – a 'phone or a tablet/laptop?</u>

Again, it depends whichever makes you feel more comfortable. Both the desktop and mobile application experiences of video interviewing have been designed with the candidate in mind – they're engaging and easy to use.

Over 25% of Sonru candidates now complete their interview on a mobile or tablet device, making video interviewing even more convenient for the candidate.

Sounds obvious but make sure that you have fully charged your laptop or mobile device, and turned off all notifications and applications. Don't leave it until the last minute to test your equipment.

3. Should I keep my glasses on?

Yes, but make sure they are clean! The interviewer wants to see the real you. It's really important to dress as you would for a face-to-face interview, even though you know the recruiter will only be able to see you from the waist up!

It may be tempting to wear your most comfortable sweats and a crisp white blouse, but dressing formally will actually make you feel more confident and assertive. Even your body language will change. This will ultimately affect your interview performance. Try to avoid busy patterns and crazy designs, instead opting for a block colour.

(**Note from Gwyneth**: if you wear glasses make sure that you are not sitting opposite a window which could cause a reflection.)

4. How much of 'me' should be on camera? My head and shoulders or more?

Your head and shoulders are perfect. Have your laptop at eye-level, so that you aren't looking down at the camera (put books underneath it to elevate as necessary) and put a desk lamp nearby so you can adjust the light.

Your viewing environment should be quiet, simple and well illuminated.

Make sure that the area your recruiter will see on video is clean and tidy. Don't sit with a window right behind you – it'll create a shadow and make you very hard to see.

5. Can I have notes in front of me?

It's a good idea to have some notes with you; it'll help calm your nerves. Only make use of your notes during the time allocated to read the questions, which isn't recorded. Looking at notes when answering your questions might show a lack of knowledge and confidence to the recruiter.

6. What if I make a mistake?

You're human! Recruiters don't expect you to be perfect. They expect mistakes, as they would in a face-to-face interview. Small mistakes are normal and nothing to worry about - you have two minutes at the end of your interview where you can add any extra comments.

Of course, some things are out of your control. If your dog Fido jumps on your lap with his loudest squeaky toy and messes up your interview, don't worry.

7. What is the difference between a video interview and a face-to-face interview?

The main difference between a video interview and a face-to-face interview is that a video interview is online. A video interview aims to recreate the same environment as a face-to-face interview.

Candidates do not see questions in advance, cannot stop, pause or re-do once the interview has started. A video interview allows candidates to show recruiters their personality and drive much earlier in the process, making sure that the most suitable candidates are invited to face-to-face interviews.

8. What does a fantastic video interview include?

To me, a fantastic video interview is one where it is clear that the candidate is relaxed and at ease with the process. Although video interviewing is a new experience for a lot of candidates, practice and research can help you have a fantastic video interview. Know the company and the job spec, research the interview process and above all, practice. This is your chance to show the recruiter what makes you tick and why you are the perfect person for this job.

9. What is your number one piece of advice to someone doing a video interview/using Sonru for the first time?

My number one piece of advice for anyone completing a video interview is to practice. As with everything, practice makes perfect. People are becoming more and more familiar and comfortable with video interview technology, thanks to mainstream social applications like Skype, Facetime and even Snapchat!

Pick a time that suits you to complete your interview and then put aside time to practise. Practise, practise and practise again. You'll gain more confidence with each practice interview and you'll ooze coolness when completing the real deal.

Thank you Sonru !!

REMEMBER – you want to do well, and everything you can do beforehand to reduce your stress levels will contribute to a better presentation.

CHAPTER FIVE - COUNTDOWN

"Before everything else, getting ready is the secret of success." – Henry Ford

When you are preparing for an interview you may be so focused on the talking part that you forget about the other, more practical arrangements.

These are equally as important however, because by eliminating all potential sources of stress, you are setting the stage for the best interview ever.

Social media

Check your social media sites and take a look at the photographs you have there. Is there one of you lifting a glass of champagne with a silly hat on your head? You may have been at your Granny's birthday party and everyone who knows you will be able to put your picture into context, but a stranger will not.

Forget about the fact that you are not 'friends' with your future employer and that they cannot see your personal information. If they want to find out about you before the interview, they will find a way.

From now on, if you would not be prepared to read what you post on the front page of a newspaper, don't post it or email it.

You could also google yourself and find out what information is available when other people search for you online.

What are you going to wear?

A very popular topic for discussion. Because I work with a wide variety of people from different educational and cultural backgrounds, some of my workshop participants might be applying for a job as an IT helpdesk operator, and some may have their eyes set on becoming CEO for a company of 1000.

When it comes to dressing for an interview, the thing is this: It doesn't matter what you are going to be wearing when you are doing the job. Your daily 'uniform' might be a t-shirt and jeans, or a suit and tie. *But you don't have the job yet*, and you want to be noticed and make a good impression.

Now I'm not suggesting for one minute that you rush out and buy an expensive suit if you are never going to wear it ever again. Apart from anything else you could end up fidgeting around on your chair during the interview because you feel uncomfortable.

But at the very least, and this applies to both ladies and gentlemen, find yourself a smart shirt to wear (with trousers or a skirt), and ideally a jacket as well.

Keep colours neutral; smart jeans have become acceptable for a number of professions, but just because you love your red shoes or green trousers or yellow shirt, it doesn't mean that the person interviewing you will (remember to check the company website and look at what people are wearing there).

If, say, five people are being interviewed for a job that involves a lot of hands-on work and all the other candidates turn up in their jeans and t-shirts, and you arrive with a clean shirt and jacket, who do you think is going to stand out?

If you make an effort with your appearance you are telling you potential employer that you are serious about wanting the job. Your appearance counts.

When you have decided what you are going to wear, check that it is clean, well in advance of your big day.

Other items on your check list should include clean shoes and tidy hair (really hope I'm not being too obvious here).

All of the above also applies to preparing for a video interview. You need to prepare exactly as if you were going to be in the same room as your interviewers.

Where are you going?

A few years ago I was invited to interview at a large organization. Fortunately I had allowed myself some extra time for taking some deep breaths before going in, which was just as well because the building where the organization was located had *five* entrances, and I didn't know which one to use.

I got to the interview with only seconds to spare and as a result the interview was awful (I didn't get the job). Find out exactly where you need to be and how long it is going to take you to get there.

How are you going to get there?

When you are planning your journey to your interview think about which mode of transport you are going to use: public transport, taxi, or car? If you are already working in the building, make sure that you know where the interview is going to be held.

Have a trial run getting there and remember to add on extra time if your interview is scheduled in the morning or afternoon rush-hour periods.

If you are driving, where are you going to park? Will you need small money/coins to pay for a car park or parking meter? You do not want to be in your interview worrying about whether you are going to get a parking ticket.

How are you going to act/behave? Practise!

What will your first words of introduction be? How are you going to say them? Will you shake hands? Practise, and practise some more.

a)   When practising your answers, refrain from using slang such as 'the guys' or 'the girls'. Use words such as 'colleagues', or 'co-workers', or 'team'. If you practise *before* the interview, the less likely you will come across as being too informal *at the interview*.

b)   Remember that one of the aims of an interview is for you to market yourself. If you are usually a little shy about telling people how great you are, get comfortable with feeling ever so slightly *uncomfortable* talking about yourself. I usually suggest to people that they take it up one level from their day to day style of conversation.

c)   *Never, ever* criticise others, even if you think that they were the most lazy or most disagreeable colleagues/boss you ever had. Two things will happen.

Firstly, you will take the interviewer's attention away from *your* good points, and secondly, you will cause them to wonder how loyal you will be.

EXERCISE

Practise walking into a room, and smile. If you don't know anyone you trust enough to practise with, spend time in front of a mirror answering your questions, or if you have a video facility on your mobile 'phone, record yourself and then watch your body language and facial expressions.

CHAPTER SIX – THE DAY

"Luck is what happens when preparation meets opportunity." – Seneca

The big day has arrived and you have worked hard to prepare all your answers so that you are going to come across as a confident and knowledgeable candidate, who will shine so brightly that the interview panel has a clear choice: *you*.

Smoking: There is nothing worse for people sitting in a smoke-free office than for someone to walk in smelling of cigarettes (or cigars). If you cannot survive without nicotine, refrain from smoking for at least half an hour before the interview, and ideally longer. Get some chewing gum!

Caffeine: You may well be a little nervous, but please take heed. Caffeine and adrenaline can cause a chemical reaction that results in panic.

Limit your caffeine intake on the big day. The last thing you want is to get to the interview and not be able to talk because your heart is pumping so hard.

Relax: Go into the washroom a few minutes before your interview is due and stretch your facial muscles. Breathe deeply three times, make silly faces at yourself in the mirror, or smile at the ceiling, whatever it takes to reduce any tension in your jaws.

Mobile phone: Turn it off.

It's ok to be nervous but *remember to breathe*! Relax and shine. Your future employer is looking for a human being who will fit in, and that could be you.

The first 30 seconds count!

Most cultures in the west prefer eye contact. Walk into the room with your head held high, shoulders back, and smile.

If you're on video, smile for a second or two before you start talking.

Acknowledge each of the panellists by greeting them, and if it is appropriate, shake hands with each one (if there is a huge table in front of you then of course you do not want to be lying across it to shake hands, but if it is just a desk or small table then make the effort).

Whilst it is highly unlikely that those interviewing you will make a decision based upon purely how you make your entrance or start your recording on screen, your manner *will* influence their attitude. These are the statistics.

Fifty-five per cent of the first impression is based upon appearance and behaviour which includes how you walk – whether you are slouching or standing up straight – what you are wearing, your body language, and your facial expressions. If you are on video you lose most of that – so SMILE !

Thirty-eight per cent of the first impression relates to *how* you speak – if you are a naturally quiet speaker then you will have to practise increasing your volume and the reverse if you tend to speak very loudly. The *words you speak will make up a measly seven per cent* of the impression that you make in those first 30 seconds.

Even if the interviewer(s) are relaxing back in their chair, have their feet on the table, arms crossed, whatever, make sure that you sit up straight, hands in your lap or in front of you.

If you are offered something to drink, my advice is to politely decline. I have seen interviewees send their glass of water or cup of coffee flying across the table or onto the floor because they have started to wave their arms around whilst describing something.

If there is a drink already on the table in front of you, move it to the side out of arm's length way. Spilling a drink could be more than your nerves can bear.

The end of the interview

Keep it simple and polite, for example:

"I look forward to hearing from you."

"It's been a pleasure to meet you, thank you for your time."

CHAPTER SEVEN - AFTERWARDS

"You don't learn to walk by following rules, you learn by doing, and by falling over." – Richard Branson

Well done, you did brilliantly!

When you finish your interview, make time to sit quietly somewhere for 10 or 15 minutes and ask yourself what went really well, what didn't go so well, and what you would do differently next time.   And then go and celebrate.

Sometimes my clients tell me that there was something they hadn't felt comfortable with, or they wished they had answered a question differently, but couldn't remember exactly what it was.

By taking time immediately after the interview, you can help yourself in the future, so that your presentation becomes even more polished. Write down your thoughts so that you have a reliable record.

You might also consider writing a quick email to the HR person with whom you have been in contact to thank them for arranging the interview. This suggestion always provokes discussion in my workshops!

If (and sometimes it happens) you are not selected for the job and you apply for another vacancy at the same company or organization at a later date, how could you ensure that the HR Office remembers you?

Regrettably it is so rare these days for a candidate to take the time to thank the person who wrote all the emails and arranged for job applications to be distributed to the right people, that if you say "thank you," the next time they see your application a little bell will go off in their head and your CV could be put on to the interview pile again.

Contrary to what some people believe, writing to say thank you will not impact the outcome of your interview.

Unless interviews are being held over several weeks, by the time you have sent your email, a decision on selection will already have been made.

Feedback

If your interview is not successful and you want to know why, you may decide to write to the company and ask for their feedback. If you do so, please prepare to be offended.

Although I'm a great fan of reflective learning, regardless of how objective the person providing your feedback believes they have been, what it will usually come down to is that you simply were not the right 'fit'.

That can be extremely difficult for them to put into words, and very demoralising for you.

Remember that you were invited for interview, and therefore on paper your experience and qualifications matched the requirements of the job. Something just didn't click. Onwards and upwards.

CHAPTER EIGHT – MONEY

"Money does not make you happy but it quiets the nerves."
– Sean O'Casey

What are your salary expectations? This is a question dreaded by many, but only because they have not taken the time to think about what they want. It may come at the interview, or it may come before the formal job offer.

You want to be paid well to do the job that you are applying for, and nobody is expecting you to work for free (at least I hope they aren't). Do you know how much you want to earn? How much do you think you are worth?

If the range of salary is not included in the job advertisement, it's time for some more research. How can you get information on the company's salary levels? What do people in similar positions get paid elsewhere?

If you can't find anything that is going to help you, you could think about how much you need to earn in order to be able to pay all the bills, then think about a salary that would pay for luxury holidays, a great car, and all the clothes/shoes/ electronic equipment, and settle on a figure somewhere in between the two extremes.

If you *are* asked the above question, these are a few of the possible outcomes:

a)   You tell the interviewer how much you want to be paid, the interviewer says thank you and makes a note but gives no indication about whether the amount is acceptable or not.

b)   The interviewer does not respond to your answer, you get nervous and so you ask them a question along the lines of "what is the range of salary that you are offering," and then they give you a figure that is far below what you had expected. You leave your interview disappointed and questioning your ability.

c)   You tell them that the job is very important to you and that you would rather only talk about salary if they are going to offer you the position.

None of these are ideal, and there is no right or wrong way to handle this situation because so much will depend upon the job that you are applying for, and how you think the interview has gone this far.

But you don't want to run the risk of ruining your chances of being offered the job, and you have only got this one opportunity to leave a good impression.

It's up to you to judge the situation, and a non-committal response that reduces pressure on both sides could be for you to say: "I have done some research and have seen that similar positions pay between xxx and xxx.

"In light of my qualifications and work experience I am looking at somewhere between those two figures" (or at the lower end, or at the higher end). The key is to be realistic, and be fair to yourself and the person interviewing you.

If you are offered considerably less than you had hoped for you could negotiate. For example you could say something like "this job is really important to me and I want to accept, but could we talk about salary again in six/12 months"?

If you have nerves of steel, when given a figure that you are not sure about, say nothing and see what happens. If you are lucky the person you are talking to may increase the offer out of sheer embarrassment.

Remember that from a business/ budgetary perspective most employers will want to pay as little as they can. That doesn't mean to say that you should sell yourself far below the going rate, rather that you should be able to recognize a fair offer when made.

If an employer is offering a very low salary and is closed to any future renegotiation once you have proved yourself, you may be better off declining the offer. Some companies are more interested in their budget line than getting the right person for the job and only you will know what you are willing to accept.

CHAPTER NINE – WHAT'S NEXT …

Be wary of telling your colleagues about your job search and interview. Human beings love to communicate with each other, and gossip and rumours quickly spread in the work environment. One scenario is that your boss finds out that you are thinking of leaving before you have a new job offer, which could be embarrassing to say the least.

When you get the job, resign in person with your line manager/direct supervisor, and then send formal written notice. There is a proverb in many languages that says that "you always meet twice in life."

You may find that your current employer asks you to stay with the offer of more money and/or additional benefits. My advice here is to think very carefully about *why* you decided to apply for another job, and to then keep going in the direction you have chosen for yourself.

If you stay, two things will happen:

- Your working relationships with your colleagues won't be the same because everyone will have judged you for wanting to leave the team …

- The other company will judge you for having wasted their time and depending on the sector you're working in, you could find yourself with a lot of burned bridges and broken connections.

One more thing.

If you spend your last days and hours in your current position, criticising your colleagues and telling everyone how you could have done a much better job than the boss, when they see your name on an application a few years later, you will most likely not even make it to interview.

Leave on a friendly note, and mention that you look forward to staying in touch.

THAT'S THE HARD WORK DONE. GOOD LUCK!

MORE QUESTIONS AND ANSWERS

In this final chapter I have put together the questions that I am asked most frequently, together with my answers.

Question:
Is it ok to tell jokes in the interview?
Answer:
If you were the person on the other side of the table and it was your money being spent on salaries, would you want to hear jokes at the interview? I wouldn't, so my answer to this is 'no' – unless of course you are interviewing for a comedy show.

Question:
What is a behavioural/competency based interview question?
Answer:
These types of questions ask you to respond by including a real-life example of the situation being referred to. So: "give me an example of when you made a mistake." You should already have relevant examples for all the answers you have prepared.

Question:
What should I do if my mind goes blank?
Answer:
Relax. You can bide your time by doing a couple of things.

Firstly ask the interviewer to repeat the question, and if necessary summarise back to them what they have just asked, to clarify that you have understood. For example, if the interviewer says "tell me about your greatest achievement", and for a second you freeze, you could say "do you mean, what was the best thing I did at my previous job?"

Another option is to say – slowly – "that is a very interesting question, thank you." If you have prepared properly, you should be able to get back on track very quickly.

Question:
Should I tell the truth?
Answer:
ALWAYS!

Question:
Should I take my references and certificates with me to the interview?
Answer:
If you feel more comfortable having your references and certificates at the ready, then take them with you. But do not offer to show them unless you are asked to do so.

Question:
There are gaps in my CV because I was unemployed. What explanation should I give?
Answer:
If you were unemployed because of redundancy as a result of restructuring, merger, etc., you can explain this to the interviewer. But then you must also describe what you have been doing during the time in question.

You might say that you have been using the time to continue your professional development, researching the job market, and networking (even if that meant lots of cups of coffee whilst reading the newspaper). Did you do any volunteering or community work? Get the idea?

Do not spend a long time explaining yourself. Remember that you have been asked to come to the interview because the company liked your application. Focus on the positive and tell the interviewer how much you are looking forward to this great opportunity.

Question:
I was ill for a long time so wasn't working. Should I give an explanation?
Answer:
Giving an answer about employment gaps because of illness can be tricky because unless your illness is going to affect your capacity to do the job, you are probably not going to want to share your personal health issues with a group of strangers.

Furthermore, employers must be very careful with these questions so as to not land themselves with an employment tribunal. You might suggest that you would be happy to share the relevant information if a job offer was on the table.

ABOUT THE AUTHOR

GwynethEL is the owner of Feelgood Coaching and Consulting, using emotional intelligence to create brilliance.

In addition to her formal university studies she is a qualified coach, and provides specialist coaching and consultancy services to show her clients how define their own brand so that they transform how they market themselves.

Gwyneth loves working with people – as opposed to machines - recognizing that each one of us is unique and is capable of creating a fabulous future according to our own values and desires.

The training and professional development of others has always been an integral part of Gwyneth's working life. She has over 25 years' experience within multi-national and multi-cultural environments such as the UN and the OSCE throughout Europe and the Balkans, as well as having worked in the private sector.

Giving back
The way that we communicate with each other is changing faster than most people can keep up with, and young people in particular face huge challenges, especially when entering the job market. Gwyneth dedicates some of her time to work with youth, helping them learn about how to support themselves and others, and to define achievable goals that will take them to where they want to be.